Released

From Dark Pit to Life with Abundant Hope

Melissa Schrock

Published by: Create Disciples Press
www.CreateDisciples.com

Print Edition: 1.0
ISBN-13: 978-0-9842733-1-7

Printed in the United States of America
May 2021

To my cousin David who lost the battle with the darkness.

To all those loved ones who could not see any light or hope.

For those who are in the pit right now.
Those hurting and crying for help.

Table of Contents

A Letter to the Reader

Thank you for picking up this book, for opening its pages, and walking into a journey of finding freedom, light, and release. These pages hold some dark days, but they are weaved with hope and light. My desire in sharing my story is to encourage and strengthen others who are walking in darkness. My heart is for God's love and redemption to blanket you on this journey. Hope is difficult to grasp and understand especially when we are walking in despair and darkness. So if you cannot see hope, then I ask you to look for light. Look for those flickers and sparks that shine a little light where you are, no matter how black.

This story covers almost a decade of my life from 2008 to 2017 although for context I do give some glimpses into the past. Laced in between the chapters, I have included poems I wrote along the way. Writing was a way for me to process my emotions and thoughts. Placing the poems between the chapters gives another frame of an upward climb to hope and light.

"Yet you, Lord, are our Father. We are the clay, you are the potter; we are all the work of your hand."

Isaiah 64:8 NIV

I am sharing with you a piece of me. While it is a part of me, it does not define me. It is a part of the precious work God is forming. I am thankful for it because without it, a piece of me would be missing. This part of me has been difficult to process and accept, but I am the clay not the Potter. The Potter knows what He is forming; He knows what I am becoming. He sees the beauty of me now, and He sees the beauty later. My vision is small, so I trust the Potter's hands.

As you walk into these pages, I am praying for you. Praying God would speak into your heart in just the way you need, and that you would experience the Sonlight in your life to gently lift you out of the dark.

Because of His love and light,
Melissa Schrock

INTRODUCTION

The Dark Pit

This is the message which we have heard from Him and declare to you, that God is light and in Him is no darkness at all.

1 John 1:5 NKJV

Dark. Deep, dark pit. Cold. Black.

Trapped. No light. No hope.

The closest thing to Hell she had ever felt.

Alone. Helpless. No strength. No life.

In a growing rural town sat a small five-tenant, brick apartment building in the center of the town's quiet streets. Inside, a twenty-year-old woman in the height of her young life was immersed in the depths of darkness. Stuck in a suffocatingly dark pit. Despair. Life had been sucked out. All life and hope held as dirt trapped in the cylinders of a vacuum cleaner. The bedroom walls were sterile and bare. Blood stains streaked across the pillow. Knives caked with dried blood were tucked in hiding under the plain, neatly made bed. On the floor the young body lay. Squeaking with her last bits of energy, calling to the God she knew was there but never felt near. *"Help, Jesus. Help."*

That young woman was me. I lived in that dark place for many years. Somehow in the midst of that place there was a God listening to my weak cries. A God tenderly working out my redemption story that led to release. Release from the dark pit of despair, one flicker of hope, one small ray of Sonshine at a time into freedom through the Son, Jesus.

The thief comes only to steal and kill and destroy. I came that they may have life and have it abundantly.

John 10:10 ESV

Will you step into this journey with me? Will you walk close to the darkness in order to see the release into freedom? Will you experience the power outside of the darkness? This is not a pretty picture of instantaneous release (though I do believe that does happen for some). This is a slow climb. A battle for release. Crying for help from the Almighty. It was excruciating. The hearts of those that loved me along the way ached. It was ugly. However, God was painting a beautiful picture I could not yet see.

These pages are filled with *"Aha!"* moments. The moments where God's radiant light shined into my dark, depressed soul. Small sparks, twinkles, flashes, and rays in the form of moments of hope, moments of healing, moments of slow release. In order to see the joy of the light and release, I will also share the dark ones. Temptation, addiction, and depression are not a lighthearted game but a battle, an all-out war. What is this war? It is for our souls. There is a fallen angel who relentlessly pursues God's people. Battles are happening. Some parts we can see while the rest remains hidden to our human eyes. Yet, there is a God willing to fight in every battle if only we ask Him.

For the Lord your God is the one who goes with you to fight for you against your enemies to give you victory.

Deuteronomy 20:4 NIV

CHAPTER 1

Darkness Falls

When you pass through the waters, I will be with you; and when you pass through the rivers, they will not sweep over you. When you walk through the fire, you will not be burned; the flames will not set you ablaze.

Isaiah 43:2 NIV

My childhood was relatively normal, nothing fancy and nothing horrific. Just everyday life lived out on a small, dairy farm. My family was hard working and dedicated. We were reserved and passive yet caring and loyal. The farm was my playground. I loved the fresh air, manure on my boots, and cow slobber on my shoulder. I enjoyed straw bale forts, sledding on the barn hill, and making mud pies. I was an average country girl. My family faithfully went to church. We had good morals and tried to serve God the best we knew how. Life wasn't easy on the farm, but it was good.

I had given my heart to Jesus at fifteen, repented of my sins, and made restitution with those I had wronged. I prayed, read the Bible, and quit participating in the things of this world. I was baptized and became a member of the church. Even though I had checked all the spiritual boxes and was the good, little, Christian girl, something was still missing.

By the time I was eighteen, I was mildly depressed and feeling lonely, worthless, and unwanted. The things that once brought happiness no longer did. I withdrew from friends as I felt I didn't fit in anyway. I abstained from sports, dating, dances, and other normal high school activities with the hope of remaining pure and unspotted from the world. I knew those activities were not the root of my loneliness and depression. During the two years as a Christian, I appreciated the life of holiness. A life free of the roller coasters I saw my friends experiencing. Yet deep inside me remained a hole, a void. If I was doing everything a good Christian should, then why was I not whole? Why did I feel empty, void, and invaluable?

One year after high school I decided to move more than three hundred miles from home to pursue a career in dental hygiene. This move was inspired by a longing for a career, and to become independent and self-sufficient. I had two semesters of prerequisite classes before I could start the actual dental hygiene program. Since these were easier, introductory classes and I desired to pay off college as I went, I found a part-time job. My college classes took place in the morning, then in the afternoon I worked until six at a daycare. Every evening I came home to my two-bedroom apartment I shared with a friend. It was a nice, little apartment with bare walls and floor space as we didn't have the things or money to fill it up. We were delighted to have this space of our own nonetheless. We both had busy schedules and didn't see each other much. We attended different churches and were generally part of separate social circles. She also worked full time. Despite our life differences, we got along very well and were supportive and encouraging to one another.

But he said to me, "My grace is sufficient for you, for my power is made perfect in weakness."

2 Corinthians 12:9 ESV

While my academic and career goals were valuable to me, I was also on a spiritual pursuit. Something was missing and I moved to seek it out, to find the missing piece. While I moved to get a degree, I was also moving to find that wholeness. I sought after a plain, modest lifestyle. Thinking that if I checked every spiritual box and did all the outward holy things, I might find it. I might fill the hole inside me. I participated in every outwardly spiritual, holy thing: covering my head, wearing long skirts, putting my hair up modestly, refraining from entertainment, participating in hymn singings, and attending every church service.

After about a year, I realized this was not filling the hole, the void. I still felt lost, alone, and in the dark. This was not the missing piece. Inside I was struggling more fiercely with thoughts of unwantedness, filth, and suicide. I felt trapped. The darkness was falling within me, and I didn't know what to do.

One evening standing alone in my apartment, my thoughts were persistent and overwhelming. The temptation was stronger than ever. Grabbing a knife from our little kitchen, I briskly walked to my bedroom and began beating my arm directly on the largest vein over and over with the knife until the blood was a stream down my arm. In that moment I felt some kind of relief, relief from the mental and emotional anguish. As I watched the blood run down my arm, I yelled out to Satan, *"There! Are you happy now? I did it!"* I knew this behavior was wrong. I had given in that night, and it was going to be a Titanic situation to save this sinking ship.

That night was the beginning of daily cutting sessions. I hated where I was, yet it was the only relief I felt, even if temporary. To cover up the wounds I wore long sleeves in the summer or large bandages. I knew I was stuck in a dark cycle, so I reached out to the elder of the church. We talked and decided counseling might be a good option at this point. I began seeing a counselor weekly and received depression medication from a medical doctor as well. Counseling gave me some accountability, however, there were many dark days in between sessions. I was not equipped to handle the intensity of the dark alone.

The darkness was thick and suffocating. The dark was constant and persistent. The dark was deep in my heart. One night this all became very obvious. Obvious that the darkness had a strong hold.

The air was cool; the sky dark and starlit. To most,

it was a beautiful, refreshing summer evening. A typical hymn sing was taking place inside a warm inviting home. The young people from church would gather at least once a weekend in a home for fellowship and singing. It was formal, women on one side and men on the other. We would sing from the hymn books for about an hour and then snacks and socializing would follow. On this summer evening the hymn sing had wrapped up in the living room and young people were mingling throughout the home.

All evening, while singing songs of hope and redemption, I had been tormented by thoughts and feelings of rejection, filth, and despair. I had been carrying these thoughts and feelings for some time, but it seemed to be intensifying. I felt alone in a deep, dark pit.

Outside their home that evening as youthful chatter filled the air, I began to wander away from the house. It was as if I was being beckoned down the grassy hill. As I reached the bottom where the grass got long, my body collapsed. Curled up in a fetal position, my body lay for what seemed like a long time. It felt as if I was not in my body. I saw my body lying there from the view of the night stars. I could not feel or move my limbs. It was an out-of-body experience.

In the distance, I began to hear people calling my name. Their voices were laced with concern. As they searched, the elder of the church was called. Due to my previous visit with him, he knew there was reason to be unsettled.

The voices continued in the distance. I tried to move, tried to call out; my body was frozen. I still had no control.

A young man walked to the bottom of the hill and found me. He asked if I was all right. I managed to squeak out a *"yeah."* That was not convincing as I still couldn't move. Soon a few others were on either side of me helping me to stand and slowly walk back up toward the house.

I was escorted to the elder's home around the corner where it was quiet and peaceful. The people around me seemed very distressed and puzzled. A plan was set in place that night for me to have mentor families, people I could stay with and not be physically alone in the darkness. This darkness had been my reality for several months now. It no longer startled me. In reality the darkness had become my closest companion. I did not understand all the fuss and concern at that time.

I had accepted the darkness. I had opened myself up to its grip. So much darkness filled me that I had picked a date of death. I could envision it on my tombstone. The how was not yet planned, only the when.

If I were to take my life today
Would my hurt really go away?

If I were to take my life today
What would my family and friends say?

If I were to take my life today
Would my true purpose be fulfilled?

If I were to take my life today
What future would I delay?

If I were to take my life today
Could God still take me as His child?

If I were to take my life today
Would my hurt really go away?

Temptation Turned Addiction

For I am convinced that neither death nor life, neither angels nor demons, neither the present nor the future, nor any powers, neither height nor depth, nor anything else in all creation, will be able to separate us from the love of God that is in Christ Jesus our Lord.

Romans 8:38-39 NIV

The daily drive to cut grew stronger. It wasn't so much the act, but the relief I craved. Somehow the pain and sight of blood caused my mind and body to relax with momentary freedom. It was like every time the skin split open a little mental and emotional pain would bleed out. Daily, and sometimes multiple times a day, the knife blade penetrated my arm.

The temptation escalated to the point of desperation. If I needed relief and did not have a knife, I used other objects to commit the act. No matter where I was, whether at work, college, a friend's house, or church, all I could think about was cutting. Things like paper clips, utility knives, razor blades, and scissors made their way across my arm in moments of complete distress. Cutting was no longer just a temptation; it was an addiction.

I had grown up watching my alcoholic and drug addicted extended family. Over and over I witnessed the pain, agony, and damage a false hope could bring upon not only the addict, but also the people that loved them. As a child I had despised my extended family. I hated how they tore everyone and everything apart for a bottle or some powder and a high. I did not get it.

And the Lord, He is the One who goes before you. He will be with you, He will not leave you nor forsake you; do not fear nor be dismayed.

Deuteronomy 31:8 NKJV

Sometime shortly after moving away from home, I began writing letters to my uncle in prison. He was addicted to alcohol and drugs, and I had felt sorry for him. Stealing, lying, and manipulating had all been a part of his actions just to get the drug he needed. He hurt my family immensely, yet through all that I felt a deep ache that I didn't understand. One evening I sat on the concrete sidewalk outside the apartment building as we talked on the phone. This was a rare occurrence as we didn't normally talk over the phone. Looking back now, I can see how God used this conversation as one of the first small breakthroughs, a moment of flickering light in the darkness, a little Sonshine.

As I talked with my uncle, I realized for the first time that I was an addict too. Addicted to a false hope. Hungry for relief from something that could and would never fully satisfy.

Sitting there on the rough concrete, I saw the other side. I felt the torment of needing something one more time. The constant thought of that thing. Knowing you are trapped yet not seeing the way out. Not seeing true hope or full light. Becoming numb to how it is affecting those around you.

Addiction keeps one in chains, locked in a dark place. This truth about where I was became a God light. Just enough light to keep my head above the waters. Just enough hope. Not a freedom or a way out, but a flicker of light for just where I was at on this journey.

CHAPTER 3

Head Spinning Lies

I can never escape from your Spirit!
I can never get away from your presence!
If I go up to heaven, you are there;
if I go down to the grave, you are there.
If I ride the wings of the morning,
if I dwell by the farthest oceans,
even there your hand will guide me,
and your strength will support me.
I could ask the darkness to hide me
and the light around me to become night—
but even in darkness I cannot hide from you.
To you the night shines as bright as day.
Darkness and light are the same to you.

Psalm 139:7-12 NLT

The storm continued in my mind and heart. The waves crashed; rocks of hopelessness stabbed my heart deep. Waves nearly drowned me in waters of lies. Lies that said, *"You are nothing; you are a disgrace; you are ugly; you are unwanted; you are fat; and you are the stain of the pure white church.*" Over and over, day after day, I was not only in the darkness; I was drowning in a sea of Satan's lies. I could not see the truth. For a time, the hope of light was gone.

I had tried so hard to be the good Christian girl. I checked all the boxes. Outwardly, I looked like I was doing good. I followed the traditions, yet my heart was dark. I felt like a disgrace and a black spot on the church. Every time I stepped into its four brick walls, I felt condemned. Not by a person, but by something within me.

For years I had struggled with body image. As a fifth grader I was taller than most other kids in my class. I was thin, yet my tallness made me feel big and fat. Despite the fact that people told me I was skinny, I felt big.

I know we often hear about the destruction of being told and labeled as fat. Of course it is painful and damaging. As a child, it is difficult to process someone being displeased with you because of your looks, your weight. Come with me for a moment to the other side. Have you ever thought about the impact of calling a child skinny? Is there a difference between *"You are fat"* and *"You are skinny?"* Are either statements positive or helpful? I venture to say no. Most people who called me skinny in my childhood and young adult years did so in a despising or derogatory manner. Hearing skinny over and over became a label that formed my identity.

After high school when I began to gain a little weight, I became fearful. I could not put it into words at the time, but I felt I was losing my identity. Another lie that added into the mix of lies raging in my mind and heart.

With this storm of emotional and spiritual lies and misplaced identity warring inside of me, I was breaking. My thoughts and judgments were skewed. One day the weight became too much. The raging thoughts swirled like a tornado inside of me, and there was no off-switch. I could not stop it. Standing in the kitchen of the apartment, I poured out a handful of depression pills and swallowed them down. Making my way back to the bedroom, I crashed on the soft carpeted floor for several hours.

Slowly opening my eyes and looking around, my brain was in a fog and my body lethargic. Somehow, through the fog I managed to remember I had piano lessons. The twenty minute drive was odd. I felt slow and in a daze, yet I miraculously made it to my destination. Inside I sat at the piano, plunking a few keys until I started feeling nauseous. Perched on the bathroom floor of my piano teacher's home I realized I was entering another level of darkness. What was happening? What was I doing? I didn't want to live like this, in this foggy, disoriented world. My pain was minimal here; however, I could not function like this. My body would not be able to work any job filled up with drugs. Cutting wasn't enough to numb the pain anymore. Yet I discovered that day I could not and would not live in the overdose fog.

God was there with me that day. He kept me and others safe on the roads. God gave me another gleam of Sonshine. He gave me the power to see overdosing was not a way out but a way farther down into the pit.

Have you ever fallen
Fallen into Satan's un-trap?

Have you ever felt lost
Burdened and alone in his un-cave?

Have you ever been surrounded
In the dark, cool un-pit?

Satan pushes, pulls, and drops
Into un-traps, caves and pits

Unworthy, unlovable, unuseful...
Have you been there?
Are you there now?

Don't let Satan rob you
Of what God has given

Worth, love, and purpose
Are yours!

He's given them as gifts
He has written your name

You are the daughter of the King
Not the slave to the thief

Kick, scream, fight your way out
Of every un-trap, cave, and pit

You don't belong in those places
You belong in the Palace
For you are the daughter of the King!

CHAPTER 4

Stripped Away

Confess your sins to each other and pray for each other so that you may be healed. The earnest prayer of a righteous person has great power and produces wonderful results.

James 5:16 NLT

Through the church family and by the grace of God, I had friends and mentors alongside me in this season. They may not have known of it all, all the pain and struggles, but what they could see was the darkness.

I believe these dear ladies prayed me out of the pit of Hell. They interceded on my behalf. I never heard them pray for me; I just felt it. The power of prayer moved on my heart and situation. Satan was making his way in; however, the power of prayer is stronger than any hold he has on us. God is touched and moved by prayer. God loves fiercely and conquers darkness every time.

As my cutting became more and more difficult to hide, people grew more and more concerned. It all came to a head when I admitted to a mentor of my multiple cutting sessions in one day. I was taken to the hospital on a cool, October evening. After spending the entire night in the ER, the hospital admitted me. I spent the next week on the psych floor.

This twenty-year-old, rural-raised girl was not *"in Kansas anymore."* People from all ages and stages shared the floor and common rooms. Varying disorders walked the halls: people who had been struggling for decades, others for just a short time. Yet we all had something in common: a dark pit of anguish. We were all stuck in this place of no light. All hopeless. All hurting from within. Being in that hospital opened my eyes to a world of psychiatric disorders and internal chains. A mother depressed and overwhelmed, a girl violated by her mentor and pastor, a man homeless and hopeless, a depressed and bedridden elderly man with Parkinson's, a woman with a horrific childhood, a girl raped by her boyfriend, a drug addicted young woman with schizophrenia. The list goes on. People held in a dark place by internal chains of pain.

For there is one God and one mediator between God and mankind, the man Christ Jesus.

1 Timothy 2:5 NIV

Through this fight I saw these chains are not easily broken. These chains may be placed on in one moment, but they can take a lifetime to remove. First light needs to come through; then the chains unlock; and finally healing follows. Release is a process. Release is a battle of fight, fall, baby steps, and letting go.

Even though my journey was nowhere near complete. Even though I still had a long road to release, in that hospital I saw another God Sonshine. In the midst of such dire circumstances I saw and felt like God was doing something. One night as I talked on the phone with my roommate, I remember telling her that God had a purpose in all this. She was amazed and said that most people can't see that kind of light in the depths of their struggles. I certainly did not feel that way or go on living like I was free, but in that moment I saw a spark of light, a glimmer of hope.

Due to being hospitalized for a full week, I was extremely behind in my dental hygiene courses. I was already barely making it before the unexpected week out. The first day back in the college classroom, I sat staring at a sheet of paper that was apparently a test. My face began to boil from the heat inside me. I had always been a good student. I had always been a prepared student. I did not recognize this person. I had missed so much material, yet more than that, my brain was not functioning at normal capacity. My brain was filled with despair and struggle, and I couldn't seem to process any new material. The words on the test page were just a jumbled mess. My teachers tried to extend grace and were kind to me. I was given another opportunity to do the test. I was thankful for their sympathy, yet their sympathy alone could not pull me out.

Within a week I realized I was too far gone. I just would not recover. Yes, I did time in the psych hospital, but I was not better. I was not cured. I was still in a dark place.

I made the hard decision to withdraw from all my dental hygiene courses. This reality threw me in a deeper, darker place for several weeks, and it took me years to overcome the loss. I had failed. My dream, my goal of becoming a dental hygienist was gone. Poof! Just like that! My last four semesters of college were gone, wasted. I was a failure.

Once again I had a misplaced identity problem. When my dream of becoming a dental hygienist was stripped away, I was naked in a dark pit. Nothing. Bare. Alone.

This identity crisis spiraled me further, yet God was not surprised. He was still with me. He was still working even though I could not see or feel it. His Holy Spirit was moving in and through the darkness. The Holy Spirit continued to shower me with rays of Sonshine.

Hope is dim
Faith is impossible
Trust is gone
Love is weak
That's how it feels
That's how it is
When the dark cloud surrounds

Believe in what
Trust in who
There seems to be no ground to stand on

Hope is dim
Faith is impossible
That's how it feels
That's how it is
When Satan robs

Trust is gone
Love is weak
That's how it feels
That's how it is
When these temptations come

Believe in what
Trust in who
There seems to be no ground to stand on

Hope is shining
Faith is possible
Trust is present
Love is strong
That's how it feels
That's how it is
When God is near

Believe in Christ
Trust in God
There is ground to stand on

Hope is shining
Faith is possible
That's how it feels
That's how it is
When prayer seeking

Trust is present
Love is strong
That's how it feels
That's how it is
When the truth meditating

Believe in Christ
Trust in God
There is solid ground to stand on

CHAPTER 5

A Need for Help

> *So let us come boldly to the throne of our gracious God. There we will receive his mercy, and we will find grace to help us when we need it most.*
>
> *Hebrews 4:16 NLT*

With my dreams of that season crushed, I felt more lost. Not only spiritually, now physically as well. My life had no purpose or direction. No goals of doing or becoming. The dark place closed in around me.

While the urge to cut had become less, I was so depressed I stopped eating and began forcing myself to throw up. This wasn't the first time I had purged. I had tried it a few times over the years. This time it seemed to stick. An eating disorder developed very rapidly between restricting and purging. My already thin body began dropping weight.

Thoughts of suicide started running through my head. I had been out of the hospital for one week and felt worse than when I went in. Walking out of those automatic hospital doors, I thought I would do better, be better. I thought I learned something up there on floor number seven. What I had retained quickly became very difficult to put into practice in my everyday life.

It was late, and the world was dark and quiet. Once again I had chosen a date of death. I lay in the darkness on my bed. My roommate knew I was in a bad place. She called over our friend next door. They tried talking to me and playing relaxing and uplifting music, but I was cold, hard, closed off. My brain was lost. My heart numb and locked tight. I was gone. Slipping away from connecting to this life. Falling from any little hope I once had. Seeing I was in a bad place, my friends called for backup. Soon the elder of the church and his wife were there in my bedroom. They began talking about bringing me to the hospital again. I was numb. I probably should have felt like a failure or tried to resist. I was too tired and engulfed by the battle. It didn't even matter anymore. Nothing mattered.

Back in the hospital I spent the next five days in scrubs and on high watch. Things were different this time. I did not see or feel any light from God. The darkness hung like a thick blanket. They started feeding me a high fat diet as I had dropped weight in just one week. Every meal included a bottle of Ensure on my tray. I could not eat. Food used to be enjoyable, but now it was a means to life. I felt no life inside me. No purpose. No value.

Eating took place in a large common room. All the patients on the psych floor came to that room for every meal. The nurses gave me strict orders not to go back to my room where the bathroom was after any meal. I tried. They did their job well as they always caught me.

By the time I left the white brick walls, I was not much better except I didn't want to end my life anymore. Due to the complexity of my depression and now eating disorder, I was referred to the Partial Hospitalization Program (PHP).

For several weeks I went to the hospital every day like I had a full-time job. It was mostly group therapy. One counselor led the discussion while five to eight of us talked through our problems. Once again I sat quietly. I was dumbfounded as to why I was there. I had grown up in a Christian home with parents who loved me and cared for my needs. Why was I in a room filled with people who had been thrown into upside-down and sideways circumstances? My life looked easy compared with most in that room. Why did I have similar symptoms with seemingly no cause?

One day the counselor pulled me aside and said, *"Melissa, don't discount what you are going through. You might not have their stories, but you are experiencing the pain."* Her words gave me comfort and relief that day. My story of how I ended up in the dark pit wasn't horrific or graphic, but that didn't make me less valuable. I had pain. I had a void. And I wasn't a failure for needing help.

Mental and emotional pain do not have a scale. There is no way to measure one's pain against another's. It is not about having a pain of ten or one. Rather, it is about recognizing you need help. Through PHP I saw another flickering Sonshine. I discovered for the first time that I did need help. I was down far, and I wasn't coming up on my own strength. I needed the help of people, resources, and most of all, God. This began my slow climb out. This acknowledgment of my pain and need, even though I didn't understand it, began a slow process to release.

CHAPTER 6

The Body, A Temple

> *Do you not know that your bodies are temples of the Holy Spirit, who is in you, whom you have received from God? You are not your own; you were bought at a price. Therefore honor God with your bodies.*
>
> 1 Corinthians 6:19-20 NIV

While the cutting had stopped, a void, a hole, a need deep inside me was still present. A piece was still missing. I did not want to stand in the darkness, yet I didn't know how to climb out. I continued to feel hurt and confused. Thoughts of suicide had subsided but I still hated me: the only person I hated and could never get away from. I felt ugly, purposeless, unworthy, and unlovable. I had dropped out of school and went from having two jobs to none. My life had been deconstructed. Everything I had been working for since moving was gone. The last fourteen months unraveled in just three weeks.

In a dark pit there is often hurt and confusion: companions in the darkness. The spiritual stuff I was doing was not helping, not growing me. I felt stale. The traditions didn't make me closer to God. Church activity and attendance didn't give me peace. I became envious of the women who flawlessly followed tradition, yet loved God and served Him. I was not finding that balance. Practicing tradition was not drawing me closer to God or allowing me to serve Him with a submissive heart. I was the Christian failure. I dropped the ball in life and wasn't doing well with faith either.

Due to raging pain and confusion, the hole inside remained. I did not want to cut anymore, but I found a replacement: purging. Purging continued even after hospital stay number two and PHP. It was my way of trying to remove the bad, ugly, failure, and unbelief. I wanted to be free. I wanted to be clean, pure, spotless. Nearly every time I ate something I went to the bathroom to throw it up. I wasn't eating much nor did I eat regular meals. I had restricted myself so firmly that my hunger signals were gone. I had destroyed my body's alert system.

When there is a void, we fill it. When there is a need, we quench it. Sometimes we use the correct remedy, and many times we don't. Our society uses entertainment, sex, drugs, porn, self-mutilation, gambling, shopping, and more to satisfy a void, a need. Why? Because we don't truly understand the void, and our need. We don't understand that it is not something we need, but someOne we need. We are not walking in the light and therefore do not see our shame. As long as we are in darkness, we cannot see, whether that is an all-consuming pit of darkness or a dark spot over a certain area of our life. We stumble until we drown in the depths of darkness or see the light.

Another ray of Sonshine came for me during a walk with a friend. I had met this friend during my first stay in the hospital. She was twenty years older than me, yet we really connected.

Green trees lined the perimeter of the park. In the center sat a vacant playground. At the edge of town it was so still and quiet. The birds sang sweetly in the distance as we walked the park's paved path. We talked and shared updates since we had seen each other last on the seventh floor.

Out of nowhere I flat out asked her if she thought I was sinning when I completed an act of self harm such as cutting or purging. She boldly told me, *"Well, the Bible says that in order to be a Christian, Jesus must be in our heart. When Jesus comes into our heart, we then become a temple of God. So if you are hurting yourself, you are damaging the temple of the living God."*

Do you not know that you are God's temple and that God's Spirit dwells in you? If anyone destroys God's temple, God will destroy him. For God's temple is holy, and you are that temple.

1 Corinthians 3:16-17 ESV

Wow. That hit me. I knew she was right. My acts of hurting my own body had great effects beyond just me. Damaging our own bodies is never just about us. It affects our relationship with God. It affects our relationship with our family and friends because suddenly we are hiding instead of being transparent. In turn, this breaks honesty and trust in the relationship. Our relationships become broken when we damage ourselves through any means in order to fill a void, a need.

This flash of God Sonshine stirred in my heart for quite some time. It didn't create immediate change. Sometimes the light needs a little more brightness to see the entire picture.

CHAPTER 7

Reframe and Renew

Do not conform to the pattern of this world, but be transformed by the renewing of your mind. Then you will be able to test and approve what God's will is—his good, pleasing and perfect will.

Romans 12:2 NIV

Through my counselor and the mentor friends around me, I was given the advice to renew my mind. At first I didn't really get it or even understand what they were encouraging me to do. Renew my mind? I knew that was in the Bible but what did it mean? How do we renew our mind? It's not like renewing our driver's license. I can't simply go somewhere and get a new copy of my mind.

Something had to change. I had been dancing with the enemy's lies long enough. Those lies were only hurting me, keeping me in a pit of despair. Freedom, release would not happen as long as I was chained and locked up by these lies. Renewal had to begin.

Over the course of the next six years I immersed myself in several methods of renewing my mind. I posted notes all over the inside of my car: truths from scripture and songs that spoke light into my dark places. Philippians 4:8 became my go-to verse. I recited it over and over. If a thought was not true, honest, just, pure, lovely, of good report, virtuous, or giving God praise, it needed to go. Kick it out. Throw it away. My counselor taught me how to reframe my thoughts. If there was a negative thought, rephrase it laced in truth. I am fat; replace it with my body is healthy. I am unwanted; God wants me and even died to have me. I am a failure; I tried, and I have learned from that mistake.

Finally, brethren, whatsoever things are true, whatsoever things are honest, whatsoever things are just, whatsoever things are pure, whatsoever things are lovely, whatsoever things are of good report; if there be any virtue, and if there be any praise, think on these things.

Philippians 4:8 KJV

Taking our thoughts captive is important in the Christian walk. We all have been there. We all have experienced the darts that threaten our mind and heart. They must be thrown into the grave. Buried and not resurrected.

When I was struggling, I would belt out a song in my car like *"Never Give Up"*. By the strength of Jesus Christ, the enemy would be put back in his place in the pit of hell. This is a war. This is a battle. We are not battling flesh. We are fighting a spiritual battle for our souls.

Looking crazy in the car is worth it when Satan loses. Because he will. In the end, he loses. God has already told us and showed us His victory.

Never give up, Never give up,
Never give up to thy sorrows,
Jesus will bid them depart;
Trust in the Lord, Trust in the Lord,
Sing when your trials are greatest,
Trust in the Lord and take heart.

Never Give Up by Fanny Crosby

Every time I sang a song, quoted a verse, or reframed my thoughts, I was choosing light. Without fail, God's Sonshine would penetrate my mind and my heart. I wasn't flawless, but I was learning the value, the practice of renewing my mind. And it wasn't a location I would go to for a new one; it was anywhere and everywhere I was in that moment: in the car, at work, at home, at a friend's house, walking down the street, night or day, I could renew my mind anytime I needed. God's truth is available all over the world 24/7.

It was killing me
From the inside out

Planted as a deceptive seed
Grew and grew to Satan's lead

So small I did not notice
Til it almost strangled me

He used my weakness
A plan to destroy

One thought
This seed

Feeding waters
In the enemy garden

Manipulation, deceit, confusion
Festered in me

It was killing me
From the inside out

Sucking life and hope
From mind and heart

Declining fast
A call for help

Only One
Could save me now

This seed small
Grew to be
A thorny vine
Surrounding me

It all started
As one thought seed
This could be the death of me

So friend do not think
On evil things
Catch them quick
Throw them back
Keep the strangling vines
From climbing in your heart

CHAPTER 8

Home to Heal

Look at the birds of the air: they neither sow nor reap nor gather into barns, and yet your heavenly Father feeds them. Are you not of more value than they?

Matthew 6:26 ESV

After much contemplation and prayer, I made the move back home. Many reasons prompted this move. Mostly I felt this was another leg on the journey. Home was the place where some of the growth and healing were going to have to take place. My roots, thought patterns, and story all began there.

Initially after high school I operated a farmstand with two of my cousins. We sold produce from an old barn on the corner of a busy intersection. The business had continued to grow after I left, so part of my move was also wrapped around this business. I was still invested and part owner. When my dad told me they were planning to expand and add a bakery, my heart jumped. Having a bakery in that little farmstand had been my dream from the start. I had imagined fresh homemade goodies sitting on shelves and the smell of delectable fruit and warm donuts blending together. I did not want to miss an opportunity to be a part of this dream and expansion.

Moving home was not going to instantly solve or even slow my problems. I still had the baggage no matter where I traveled to. Being home wasn't going to create some miraculous healing. No, this was still going to be a fight, a climb, and a journey of finding freedom.

When I moved back, I knew I needed to have a good support system and accountability, or I would just fall back again. This was one of the number one things taught in the psych hospital. Change, growth, and healing could not happen alone; there needed to be accountability, a support system.

Love is patient, love is kind. It does not envy, it does not boast, it is not proud. It does not dishonor others, it is not self-seeking, it is not easily angered, it keeps no record of wrongs. Love does not delight in evil but rejoices with the truth. It always protects, always trusts, always hopes, always perseveres.

1 Corinthians 13:4-7 NIV

For a time I lived back at the house with my parents and two older sisters. It was a little crazy having five adults under one roof, but it provided companionship. With five people in the house there was always someone home. I wasn't truly alone; therefore, it was more difficult to make bad choices. Growing up we had always eaten dinner together, and that didn't change for us as adults. Having that accountability brought me into a lifestyle of meals again. I still didn't eat a lot, and I still purged some, but it became less frequent.

A few months before I moved, my psychiatrist expressed concern. I was twenty one years old and weighed less than one hundred pounds. He threatened to send me to a type of eating disorder boot camp to help me become healthier. The program required the patient to be fully submerged in the program for months, similar to a drug rehab program. After five weeks of hospitalizations and PHP, my life had already been halted and turned upside down. I was terrified of being shipped away for months. This valid concern and threat shook me. I needed help and healing. I needed to find the key to unlock this prison pit. I became more focused on seeking help and healing.

Back at home I was able to be set up with a spiritual mentor. A woman with no formal training other than life itself. Once a week I would sit at her kitchen table with a warm cup of cappuccino. She treated me with great love and kindness. I felt like a daughter and friend in her home. She helped me open up and process my thoughts, feelings, and experiences. She never judged me for my behaviors or struggles; instead, she genuinely cared about me. She was a safe harbor in the middle of the storm. She gently brought up my weaknesses yet also reminded me I had strengths. Through her mentorship, I began experiencing love again. Love was like a warm, fuzzy blanket to my cold, shivering heart. The numbness was slowly thawing. My heart was awakening.

With her guidance, I sought out nutritional counseling. I only met with the dietitian a few times; however, her wisdom and insight were a turning point. Setting foot inside a hospital was scary as my previous experiences had been nightmarish. I walked the plain, sterile hallway looking for the nutrition office. When I arrived, I was taken into a small office space. She sat across from me at a small, round, fake wood grain table. She was gentle and kind. In a caring manner she asked me some questions to get a basic understanding of my story and why I was there. She did not give me a puzzled or disgusted look as I had experienced before. She simply listened.

The visits were filled with education and wisdom. She showed me portion size. In front of me sat a plate of fake food with the correct portion size. I stared blankly at the plate. I was eating half or less of what she had sat in front of me. It was overwhelming to think of eating more. She obviously understood this and helped me set small, achievable goals.

Through her counsel I saw a Sonshine spotlight into my darkness of distorted eating. I came to understand I had a number problem. One hundred. I hated one hundred. I did not eat foods containing more than one hundred calories. Similarly, I feared being heavier than one hundred pounds. While I never completely understood where the one hundred came from, she helped me unpack it enough to try to move on.

I later realized one hundred started back in middle school. I was told I would not start my period until I reached one hundred pounds. I dreaded starting my period. I liked the innocence of being a little girl. I had older sisters, and a period looked negative, painful, and annoying.

The day I started my period, I cried. My journey into womanhood began with tears. The foundation of being a woman began rocky and stayed that way for many years. One hundred was a locked-in number: a physical and mental barrier keeping me in bondage. The next several years became full combat in my mind, fighting to let it go and mentally being okay with a weight over one hundred pounds. I physically had to work diligently to allow my body to gain weight. I was not a little girl anymore, and I needed to move on, move past the old fears.

CHAPTER 9

Sin has Consequences

Jesus answered them, "Most assuredly, I say to you, whoever commits sin is a slave of sin."

John 8:34 NKJV

The gentle, wise woman peered over her glasses at me. While she was giving me hard truths, something about how she presented it softened my heart. I didn't feel attacked or afraid. She helped me find the courage to face it, to chip away at these twisted lies. During the few visits with the dietitian, I realized I had father issues. My dad was my hero growing up, and he still is. While my relationship with my dad is beautiful now, it wasn't always that way. In the last several years we have grown closer and share deep things of the heart. I am thankful for how much my dad and I have grown over the years, and I wouldn't trade the relationship we have now. It is precious. As a child my dad taught me the value of being kind to others and working hard. My dad was probably hard working to a fault at times. He was a busy farmer and good at what he did. I loved being with him on the farm, but that was the only time I really got to be with him. Most of the time growing up, I felt my dad was emotionally unavailable.

As it has been told, our dad experiences can play a role in our view of God, our heavenly Father. I projected unavailability onto God. I figured He didn't really want or have time for a relationship with me. I thought relationships with God were only for the super spiritual: those who could quote Scripture; those who studied the Bible every free moment, and those who dedicated their lives to the work of the Lord like pastors and missionaries. I was very wrong, and I was on a journey that was opening my eyes.

And yet, O Lord, you are our Father. We are the clay, and you are the potter. We all are formed by your hand.

Isaiah 64:8 NLT

While continuing to talk with the dietitian, she brought to the surface the damage an eating disorder was placing on my body. My esophagus was slowly getting eaten away by my own stomach acid. Every time I purged, the acid that came with it was affecting my esophagus and mouth. I had heard this before, but this time it was beginning to sink in as purging had been going on for some time.

The other damage was on my reproductive system. At the time of our visits I hadn't had a period in many years. It was likely my reproductive system was jacked up. The dietitian told me it was possible I would not be able to have children. It wasn't a big deal to me then as I didn't have any prospects or a strong desire to even get married. Yet the more I thought about it, the more I realized once again my decisions were not only affecting me. One day the man I loved would have to share my poor choices and also bear the consequences. That was not fair. Sin is never fair. Sin never affects only one.

Whoever sows to please their flesh, from the flesh will reap destruction; whoever sows to please the Spirit, from the Spirit will reap eternal life.

Galatians 6:8 NIV

After my visits with the dietitian, I became more determined to make these habits stop. I needed to let go of these false expectations of my daddy-daughter relationship. I was not that little girl anymore. My relationship with my dad could be improved. Maybe it would never be what I imagined as a girl, but it could be something better, maybe even something beautiful. My purging came to a halt. I had a new desire to heal, to do better. Someday I wanted to be healthy and well for that man: the man who would hold me and love me. Despite my attempts, restricting was still hanging on. With only my own strength I would never defeat this Goliath. Time had already shown that I needed God's light, His ray of Sonshine and an army of believers praying for me and coming alongside me.

When I'm all alone
I talk with Him
Like He's right there beside me

Sometimes I cry
And the tears trickle down my cheeks
Sometimes I shout angry words
And my heart beats fast
When I'm all alone
I talk with Him
Like He's right there beside me

Sometimes I whisper
And peacefully request
Sometimes I stand
And sing with all my heart
When I'm all alone
I talk with Him
Like He's right there beside me

Sometimes I sit
And write the words I cannot say
Sometimes I smile
And thank Him for another day
When I'm all alone
I talk with Him
Like He's right there beside me

Sometimes I bow my head
And humbly give
Sometimes I reach out
And I feel His gentle touch
When I'm all alone
I talk with Him
Like He's right there beside me

CHAPTER 10

A Choice

O Lord my God, I cried to you for help, and you restored my health. You brought me up from the grave, O Lord. You kept me from falling into the pit of death.

Psalm 30:2-3 NLT

Two of my coping mechanisms in this season were writing and reading. Back in my darkest, most depressed state I began to journal and write poems. It was a safe space to admit my pain, hurt, thoughts, emotions, and experiences. Talking about these things was difficult but writing came easy.

I filled journal after journal. No person was reading them; however, I have full confidence God heard every word. He was right there as tears rolled down my cheeks and as my pencil wrote angry words. He heard my cries, my pleas for help through these words. He heard my confessions and confusions. While it may not have looked like a traditional prayer, I was calling; Christ was interceding; and God was absolutely listening.

Prayer doesn't have to look a certain way. Sometimes

we need to get on our knees in a quiet room, undistracted. Other times it looks a little more messy. Life is messy. God understands that. He doesn't have a prayer formula. He doesn't even have a prayer condition. All come, as you are, wherever you are, come. He will never turn a soul away that comes to Him. At the time I did not understand I was praying, yet my heart did call out and plead for help over and over.

Along with writing came reading. I began a season of reading self-help books. At first it was about gaining insight and helping myself. Later it became a desire to be equipped to help others.

"Lord, help!" they cried in their trouble, and he saved them from their distress. He sent out his word and healed them, snatching them from the door of death. Let them praise the Lord for his great love and for the wonderful things he has done for them.

Psalm 107:19-21 NLT

My mentor was also a reader and suggested many books that impacted me. I specifically remember sitting on an airplane reading. The book was titled Healing is a Choice. I never even finished the book, yet the pages I did read sparked a new thought and a Sonshine in the dark. I finally realized I needed to make a choice. I needed to decide to heal or not to heal. I needed to either seek freedom or live enslaved. No one else could choose for me. No one else could just make it happen. I needed to decide. Then I needed to make decisions in life based on that choice.

If I was going to choose healing, then I needed to remove things that caused me to stray from that choice or fall back into captivity. To this day I do not have a bathroom scale. Something so simple can cause me to walk in chains again.

God calls and desires for us to live in freedom. Christ came to this earth to set the captive free; whatever that captivity looks like. Whether it is viewed as great or small, there is freedom. There is healing. And it starts with a choice. Healing is a choice you can make. Freedom is a lifestyle you can live in. Not by your own strength, but by the very power of Jesus dying on the cross.

CHAPTER 11

Universal Language

There is no fear in love, but perfect love casts out fear. For fear has to do with punishment, and whoever fears has not been perfected in love.

1 John 4:18 ESV

One day when the air was still cool, the trees bare, and the skies gray, I was driving in my car with the radio on. Music had become my soul sunshine. In the car, while I worked, and at home, music was often playing in the background. On this particular day I heard an announcement for an upcoming trip to Russia.

My heart leaped. Starting in my early teen years I had developed a heart for orphans, especially from Russia.

While doing some leisure reading when I was in seventh grade, I picked up a book from the library about the life of an orphan girl titled Nobody's Daughter. My heart was broken through those pages. I connected and ached for this unwanted girl.

Throughout the years in school, I wrote several

research papers on varying aspects of orphanages includ-
ing those in Russia. Something about that country also
broke my heart. They were a well-developed country, not
a third world by any means, yet their orphanage system
was corrupted and twisted. The orphanages were often
understaffed, leaving babies cribbed and seated in their
feces. The older kids were often abused or taken advan-
tage of. Love was rarely a part of an orphan's life. It was
a fight, a survival of the fittest. As a whole, Russia was a
depressed and oppressed country from the highest and
rich to the poorest and orphaned.

As the days went on, I continued to hear this message
on the radio. A call for people to sign up and come along
to bring love and the Good News to orphan children in
Russia. My heart was moved. I could not say no to this
opportunity. I went through the process, filled out an
application, had an interview, and then was given confir-
mation to go.

I joined over thirty others I had never met from the
radio listening area. We traveled to Russia fully equipped
with children's Bible School supplies and personal care
items for each child we would meet. Our time was spent
in three different orphanages and also included a short
visit at the orphan intake hospital. The kids were mostly
shy and unsure about us, but soon they warmed up with
the games, crafts, and activities. I had never experienced
a place where the language barrier was strong, yet it did
not intimidate the thirty plus team members or really the
kids either. This showed me the meaning behind "*actions
speak louder than words.*" Love and care can be spoken

without a single word coming from any lips. Love is not just merely words that we speak; it is rooted deeply in our hearts. I may not have been able to speak one word of Russian; however, I did speak one language the kids could understand, and that was love.

Throughout this climb out of the dark pit, I was experiencing the power and depths of love: a truth light shining into the darkest corners of my heart. Growing up in an extended family of alcoholics, drug addicts, and abusers, love became warped. These people would tell me they loved me with their lips, but their actions showed otherwise. I was beginning to see and understand that love does not lie, cheat, steal, use, or abuse. Love does not create confusion or fear. Love brings life. Love brings peace.

In many ways like these orphan kids, I was on a journey of discovering love. I was trying to define love by God's standards now. The human definition I had known was false. Human love was flawed. It had brought hurt into my life instead of healing and peace. This love I had seen and experienced was not true love. Pure, undefiled love comes only through God and those completely surrendered to Him. I had discovered some pure, genuine, loving people on this climb from the darkness. It wasn't love by their own strength or goodness. It came by the power of the Holy Spirit inside of them.

Prior to this journey, I felt uncomfortable talking about the Holy Spirit. It was the part of God I shied away from because I didn't understand or comprehend.

I thought it was something only great disciples of Jesus could have and understand.

The team I was serving with in Russia was a group of people filled with love and the Holy Spirit. I had never been surrounded by such a group in my life. The group was composed of thirty people of varying ages and different upbringings. They were thriving in a variety of denominations and didn't share the same convictions, yet they were united through the love of Jesus Christ and the power of the Holy Spirit.

I was experiencing undefinable love. A pure love that came only through the power of the Holy Spirit. God's glowing Sonshine was filling me with the real love I had been longing for. I had been an orphan to pure, undefiled love and was now given a light of hope that love did exist.

I try to put You in a box
I try to define You by what I know

I try to hear You with my ears
But You're speaking to my heart

I try to see You with my eyes
But it is my faith that will make You visible

I try to touch You with my hand
But You reach beyond my skin to hold my heart

I try to put You in a box
I try to make sense of You in my mind
But You are my Creator, my Potter

I try to understand Your love
But it is deep; it is agape

I try to put You in a box
I try to define You by what I know

But I will never truly
Understand by my human brain

It does not take knowledge to know You
Research will never discover Your mystery

God is not a box I can open, see and understand
But to know Him, to see Him
It starts with the heart
It continues with faith
And grows with acceptance

That God is not defined
By the lines and corners of a box

He is love
Alpha and Omega
Savior and King
Holy of holies

He does not wish for my definition
He knows who He is

He wishes for me to join Him
Allow Him to be Father
Trusting, believing
He will never fail

He will listen late at night
He will protect on the road

He will give strength to climb the mountain
He will comfort in the dark

For He is Father
And so much more

I will not define You anymore

CHAPTER 12

Not Alone

> *Religion that God our Father accepts as pure and faultless is this: to look after orphans and widows in their distress and to keep oneself from being polluted by the world.*
>
> *James 1:27 NIV*

It was our first evening together in Russia. We were gathered at the end of one of the hotel hallways sitting on a few chairs, the floor, and window ledges. We were bubbling with excitement and uncertainty about what the next week would hold.

As we began praising God for a safe arrival, praying for the coming week, and simply worshiping Him together, I was touched. I had never experienced a group diverse yet unified because of the working of the Spirit. How could we lay our differences aside? Love. Pure, undefiled love. Love flowing from the very heart of God into us. For the first time I felt like God was holding a watering can over my heart, and I was getting a long and refreshing drink of love.

This was one of the missing pieces. When I started

falling into the pit of despair, I did not have love. I was not experiencing the transforming, redemptive power of His love. I was walking in little faith without love. A Christian without love is a stale cracker. Sucking moisture from others. I was dried up with nothing to give and unable to receive a drink. God was bringing me out of the dry, withered state. He was giving me a drink, and I was accepting it. Living water for my thirsty soul. Refreshment for my depressed mind. The ascent was happening. I was coming out of the dark. I was finding the missing pieces I had set out to find four years prior. I was believing there was indeed hope.

Over the course of the week in Russia alongside thirty individuals, I found common ground even outside God's amazing love. One evening gathered in the space by the hotel elevators, we shared testimonies. It was a beautiful time with people real and vulnerable about what God had done and was doing in their lives. That evening I discovered I was not alone in my struggle with depression and the dark pit. There were other Christians that had experienced deep depression. It wasn't a time of pity with each other but of encouragement and hope. There was complete freedom in the love and salvation of Jesus Christ. I was seeing this darkness was not going to last. I was on an upward climb toward release. For the first time in a long time, I felt excited.

As the week progressed, I had an opportunity to share my testimony with the teenage orphans. In speaking to them, healing was settling into my heart. I finally knew I was on the road to recovery. I finally felt God's presence in and around me.

God was walking me into the light. He was opening my heart to encourage others along the way. This journey really wasn't just for me as I had expressed three years ago in the psych hospital while on the phone with my roommate. God was giving me a story to share. A story to love others through. A story of hope and love that brought me to sit at the computer in the early morning hours for months. I am sharing with you today because God's light, His Sonshine, comes in many forms and through many different avenues. Maybe, just maybe, these words and this story can give you a little light, a flicker of hope, a ray of Sonshine in your dark places and spaces.

CHAPTER 13

Authentic Relationship

For there is one God and one mediator between God and mankind, the man Christ Jesus, who gave himself as a ransom for all people.

1 Timothy 2:5-6 NIV

By the time I got back from Russia, I no longer had a desire to purge. It was gone. The greatest hurdles before me were my small portion sizes and my self-imposed dietary restrictions. Also I was still shuffling through my spiritual questions of who God was and what that looked like in my life.

After serving with the dedicated Christians in Russia, I had an interest in meeting other Christians outside my home church. I liked the church I grew up in and cared about the people, yet I felt like I wasn't growing or understanding the boundless love of God. For several months I began attending two other churches as well as going to my home church. I often went to two or three church services in one weekend. It sounds crazy, but I was hungry. Hungry for a deep relationship with God.

In this season through God's radiant Sonshine, I was discovering I could have a real, authentic relationship with God. Prior to this, I thought an intimate relationship with God was only for men and leaders in the church. I truly did not know God deeply loved me and wanted an intimate relationship with me, with every soul. Christ came and died on the cross for our sins, so we could have a relationship with God. Jesus dying and coming back three days later has given us all access to the Father, a relationship with Him. We don't need a Moses anymore. We don't need one holy man communicating between God and us. We have been given freedom to access the Throne any time.

This was monumental in my walk with God. I began praying like He was listening. I began seeking Him throughout the day. I began praising Him on my own without a church building. Finally, I was communicating with God. I had a relationship with Him. I started to feel God leading me. I was doing things I never would have done before on my own. Taking long drives and praying, giving a homeless woman my groceries, going on dates with Jesus to coffee shops, walking into a church I had never been to before, praying with and for people no matter where we were. The Holy Spirit was in my heart. The deadness I once felt was coming alive.

CHAPTER 14

True Identity

For those who are led by the Spirit of God are the children of God. The Spirit you received does not make you slaves, so that you live in fear again; rather, the Spirit you received brought about your adoption to sonship. And by him we cry, "Abba, Father." The Spirit himself testifies with our spirit that we are God's children.

Romans 8:14-16 NIV

Growing up my sister and I were often mistaken as twins even though we are two and a half years apart. We shared nearly everything as kids: a bed, a room, sometimes clothes. On the farm we shared the responsibility of taking care of the calves. We spent many hours feeding, cleaning buckets, scrubbing hutches, and of course goofing off too. We were a pair, so it was no surprise that even in my darkest season she could still make me smile and laugh.

In my bakery business she had become my right hand.

We didn't need words to communicate or understand one another. We moved around that bakery like a flowing faucet: smooth and effortless. I was grateful for her. Many times I have thought about how I would not have been successful in the bakery business without her.

When it was time for her to marry the man of her dreams, I was mixed with feelings of joy and sorrow. Happy that she was following her heart. Happy she found a steady, caring, hardworking man. Happy that she was stepping into the next chapter of her life. On the other side, I felt sad. Sad she was moving more than sixteen hours away. Sad that my bakery companion was leaving. Sad that my best friend would no longer live and work with me.

But you, O Lord, are a God merciful and gracious, slow to anger and abounding in steadfast love and faithfulness.

Psalm 86:15 ESV

During this transition, I began feeling more depressed. With the heaviness growing, I decided to go back on depression medication. I didn't want to harm myself, but I did feel tired, overwhelmed, and ready to give up on any goal or dream I was beginning to form.

Obviously I had known deep, dark depression, and I did not want to go there again. I was resisting a major fall; however, the hope and joy I had gained seemed to be slipping.

I still had struggles and bad days. I remained highly fixed on body image. I had restricted my diet severely. My *"off-limits"* food list was long. My weight remained low. On top of restricting I was also engaging in regular exercise. Exercise is good and healthy; however, my calorie intake was so low that exercise was depleting anything I had left. Exercise was another form of purging for me in that season. My struggle with body image and self-worth was keeping me from complete relief and freedom in Christ.

My mind began focusing on my failures. Peers from high school were graduating with four-year degrees and heading into master's degrees or careers. All the while, I was still living in my hometown with my family. It didn't seem to matter to me that I was part owner in a thriving business. In my mind, my life didn't look like the average or typical life of a twenty three year old.

I was still placing my value, worth, and identity in exterior circumstances. I had not yet accepted my true identity: beloved, child of God, beautiful, made righteous and pure by the blood of Jesus. I was still fighting and struggling in the pit of darkness due to my lack of faith and trust in the living, almighty God.

For God made Christ, who never sinned, to be the offering for our sin, so that we could be made right with God through Christ.

2 Corinthians 5:21 NLT

Time went on. I found a new normal without my bakery right hand. I moved out of my parents' house and in with my oldest sister. I was beginning to move past the failure. The business was successful. I was working hard. Just because life didn't look like I had planned, didn't mean I was a failure or disgrace. This ray of Sonshine allowed me to see I could let go of this unrealistic expectation I placed on myself because I was loved, valued, and growing in faith. Most importantly, I was gaining a deeper understanding of who God was and my relationship with Him.

CHAPTER 15

When God Is in It, There Is Peace

Do not be anxious about anything, but in every situation, by prayer and petition, with thanksgiving, present your requests to God. And the peace of God, which transcends all understanding, will guard your hearts and your minds in Christ Jesus.

Philippians 4:6-7 NIV

Six months after the Russia trip, I received an email from a teammate. I had only connected with her on the last night we were together in Russia. I was in her hotel room with many of the young ladies when she started to braid my hair. We talked, and I realized she wasn't as intimidating as I thought she was. All week I had seen how different our personalities were. She seemed confident; I was unsure of myself. She was loud; I was quiet. She was outgoing; I would rather fade into the background. We were different in many ways, yet we held a connection. We had walked into places rarely walked by stepping into orphanages where they saw guests maybe once a year. Our bond was only through a love God placed in our hearts.

So on this day in the dead of winter, she shared that I had been on her heart along with her brother. She felt strongly that we should communicate. I was shocked at first. I hadn't heard from her in over six months. It all seemed out of the blue to me. Also I was not in a season of looking for a spouse or even a male friendship. I was busy enough: building a business, working at a daycare, and discovering intimacy with God. Nonetheless, I told her I would be interested in communicating via email if he reached out first.

Now may the God of hope fill you with all joy and peace in believing, that you may abound in hope by the power of the Holy Spirit.

Romans 15:13 NKJV

A few months later I received that email. Later, I found out his sister pestered him for months to write to me. When he finally did, he just let it out. He didn't hold back. He really wasn't interested in a long distance relationship and was trying to scare me off. I read that email and was humorously impressed. This was obviously a man who loved God. He was honest and straightforward stating that he lived in a dilapidated trailer, worked a minimum wage job, and was mildly depressed. Normally, you would think run, run as far as you can! However, something intrigued me about this man. Something seemed different.

Our relationship started then as an emailing friendship. For the first nine months we communicated only through email. We were not distracted by presence or appearance. We were able to build a foundation without physical persuasion. This friendship was honest and genuine. It felt different than any other relationship I had ever had. The greatest key was that I prayed, and he as well, every step of the way. I did not make a decision in this relationship without covering it with prayer. I was not on a quest for the right man but on a journey of spiritual growth.

So letting your sinful nature control your mind leads to death. But letting the Spirit control your mind leads to life and peace.

Romans 8:6 NLT

One year into our friendship, I realized I was starting to have deeper feelings for him. I felt God was telling me I needed to define this relationship. I wrote to him immediately and asked him what his feelings and intentions were. If he was not invested and not interested in marriage, then I strongly felt we needed to end the relationship. I told him openly how I felt. He responded with care and love. He was interested. He was even ready to start talking about the next step.

I am generally an indecisive and slow person when it comes to decisions. Decisions have torn me up inside

many times. This time was different though. This time I
had peace and clarity. Because of my normal tendencies,
I knew this was God working in me. God brought peace
into my heart. His Sonshine left no shadow of doubt.
This was His plan. I could trust Him; I could trust the
peace. I did not understand why I needed to move more
than 500 miles away from everything I had come to know
and love, but I had peace. Peace that the relationship was
good. Peace that God was in it. Peace that I was going to
continue to grow and climb out of the dark pit.

CHAPTER 16

Reflected Love

Whoever dwells in the shelter of the Most High will rest in the shadow of the Almighty. I will say of the Lord, "He is my refuge and my fortress, my God, in whom I trust."

Psalm 91:1-2 NIV

The first years of marriage are a foundation and growth of trust. Without trust, a relationship is dead. If a husband and wife do not trust one another then communication will always be a battle zone.

Our conflicts in the first year of our marriage centered around trust. I loved my husband. I thought he was amazing. I respected him. However, we stumbled along the way because I did not fully trust him. I was afraid he would hurt or disappoint me. I was frightened he would change his mind about marrying me. I did not trust his love as real and genuine. Due to the lack of trust and the presence of fear, I did not communicate well with my husband. I assumed things rather than talk to him.

My husband owned his own business and worked from home with his office being right off the kitchen.

Working from home was still a new thing at that time, so it was a major adjustment for me. In the first months, I would make dinner and then just sit there and wait for him to come out of the office rather than communicate. I was in turn hurt because he didn't come even though he had no idea dinner was ready. Lack of trust and failing to communicate becomes a trapping cycle. When we don't trust or communicate in relationships, we can set ourselves up for repetitive hurt.

My husband was very patient. He would sit on the couch holding me waiting until I was ready to talk. It would be silent minute after minute as he waited. I would need this time to collect my thoughts, formulate my words, and gather courage. Sometimes, I even wrote to him because it was my most comfortable form of communication. As my husband waited for me countless times, he treated me with gentleness instead of frustration and anger; thereby, my heart began to soften to the reality of his real, pure, and genuine love for me. Through his love, I saw that I could trust him.

We know how much God loves us, and we have put our trust in his love. God is love, and all who live in love live in God, and God lives in them.

1 John 4:16 NLT

Even with this gentle love, there were still times of hurt. We are both imperfect humans, but what I saw was that the risk of fully loving and fully trusting was worth it. Trusting and loving my husband was worth it. He was not trying to hurt me. He cared about my heart. Mistakes happen, yet when there is a foundation of trust, the walls of the relationship will not crumble. And forgiveness can happen where there is trust.

Even after marrying a strong, gentle, patient man that loved me, my struggles did not just vanish. I still had a deep-seated problem with body image and self-worth. While I was no longer hurting myself, I brought a restricted diet into our marriage. I was still less than one hundred pounds. I knew I needed to gain weight, but I struggled doing so both physically and emotionally.

One evening in our little trailer in the woods, I was placing dinner on our new Corelle plates we had received as wedding gifts. As I placed one plate in front of my husband and the other at my spot, my husband looked up at me. First he made this laughing sound and then said, *"Honey, why is your portion much smaller than mine? It is less than half. Look!"* His comment startled me. Not because it hurt, but because I still truly did not comprehend portion size. It was a default setting. I didn't think about what I did; it was just natural to me. Eating very little was normal, natural. Not feeling hungry was natural. I was shocked. I still had a long way to go in this struggle with food and body image.

In the first years of our marriage, God used my husband as a reflection of His love, a twinkle of Sonshine. My husband's love, care, and attention to my needs was an imperfect reflection of the love of God. Staring into my husband's eyes, I saw a glimpse of Jesus smiling back into the depths of the dark places of my heart.

Even after all I had been through. After all the people that poured love into my life; and even after marrying an amazing man, love was still a hurdle on my track of life. I had an inward battle with God's love for me. I knew it. I knew in my head God loved me. God loves everyone. Yet I didn't feel it in my heart.

CHAPTER 17

Walls of False Protection Demolished

There is no fear in love, but perfect love casts out fear. For fear has to do with punishment, and whoever fears has not been perfected in love.

1 John 4:18 ESV

A little over a year into our marriage, I became pregnant with our first child. I was excited yet tense. I still felt messed up inside. How was I going to care for this little precious life and not mess it up?

During the first two months of the pregnancy, I was nervous about having a miscarriage. I knew the statistics of miscarriage and the added risk of having an eating disorder. I called on God repeatedly for His protection over this growing life inside me.

One afternoon as I was coming home from work, I stopped to fill my old Malibu with gas. Before stopping I had been thinking about the baby. Hoping for the opportunity to hold its tiny body in my arms. Standing at the gas pump, the cold, winter wind numbed my cheeks. Then in an instant, I heard from God. At this ordinary gas pump, doing a necessary task, I heard God speak right into the fear in my heart, *"She is going to be okay."*

From that moment on, I had full hope and confidence that I would give birth to this little girl growing in my womb. I was going to have the privilege of holding her in my arms. This moment was life changing; not only the impact of knowing this baby's lungs would fill with air and breathe new life, this experience also brought life into the dead places in my heart and my relationship with God. God spoke to me. Messed up me. God cared enough about my fears that His spotlight of Sonshine spoke truth and life into my heart. God cared about me! God did love me. God does speak to me. My cycle of distrust, unwanted feelings, and unacceptance of love was all breaking down. Between God Himself and my husband, my walls of false protection were tumbling. My heart was beginning to open.

I could trust my husband because he cared for me and didn't want to see me hurting. I was wanted because God sent His Son to die a cruel death, so He could speak to me personally about my daughter while she was still in my womb. I could accept love because God's love was real, authentic, and genuine. God was faithfully helping me out of the dark pit, little by little, and light by light. God was becoming my Father, and He was healing those little girl fears, wounds, and misunderstandings. God was the filling for the void. He had been what I needed all along.

Blessed is the man who trusts in the Lord, And whose hope is the Lord. For he shall be like a tree planted by the waters, Which spreads out its roots by the river, And will not fear when heat comes; But its leaf will be green, And will not be anxious in the year of drought, Nor will cease from yielding fruit.

Jeremiah 17:7-8 NKJV

I am beloved. Not just some, but everybody is beloved: beloved by our Creator, God, and Father.

My Father's arms
Hold me tighter when I am crying
Lift me up when I can't stand

My Father's arms
Reach out when I fall and stray
Link in mine to lead me on the way

My Father's arms
Are large enough to carry me
Over each stormy sea

My Father's arms
Gently correct when I turn back
Give me a nudge to continue on

My Father's arms
Show His love
Always open for me to abide

My Father's arms
Show His mercy
Closed tight to comfort and protect

My Father's arms
Are where I like to be
All secure

There is no fear
In my Father's arms
But love, comfort, security abound

So in my Father's arms
I want to stay
Although some days I run away

Sometimes the view distorted
Me, unworthy is all I see
And from my Father's arms I run

As comfort I cannot accept
Heaviness sinks in me
But as I reject
Still I find
My Father's arms open wide
Waiting patiently for me to abide

CHAPTER 18

Let Go or Drown

Remember not the former things, nor consider the things of old. Behold, I am doing a new thing; now it springs forth, do you not perceive it? I will make a way in the wilderness and rivers in the desert.

Isaiah 43:18-19 ESV

As the pregnancy continued, my body was changing. For the first time I could not control my body. I could not keep my belly from busting out of its once flat state. I could not keep my ankles from doubling in size. I could not starve and deprive my body as this meant the neglect of the life inside me. My perspectives were being forced to change. I had to let go or drown in my sin and take my baby and myself with it.

I was terrified. Afraid of becoming a mom and messing it all up. Scared to push beyond boundaries I had set up over the last ten years. Terrified to exceed one hundred on the scale. Shaken by my new intensity of hunger. And overwhelmed by my changing body from swollen ankles to enlarged breasts.

In all my fear I was seeing how small I was. Not unimportant or devalued, just small and weak. I did not have control at all! I did not have control over my changing body or my circumstances. All those years of purging and restricting food intake was all about control. I thought if I controlled my weight I could control my fears and other aspects of my life. The fears and emotions were numerous and I wanted to be in charge, not them. This was my life, right? What pregnancy taught me was how little control I had and that control really didn't profit me anything except a heavier burden. What I could control in life was my reaction, and where I put my confidence, hope, and trust. This body wasn't it. This body was going to change. However, I was coming to know someOne unchanging. SomeOne I could trust. He had already proven He is fully in love and fully committed to captivating my heart.

In Him we have redemption through His blood, the forgiveness of sins, according to the riches of His grace.

Ephesians 1:7 NKJV

My body is weak and fragile, yet my spirit can grow stronger. My spirit was being invaded by a loving, patient Father that was rocking all my false identities, self-esteem issues, and past hurts. My heart was being transformed from the inside out. His Sonshine was bright and warm like a heat lamp for baby chicks. I had read of this transformation. I knew of Paul, David, and the disciples, yet when your heart is experiencing transformation, it is like stepping at the edge of the Grand Canyon. Being overcome by the power and magnitude of what you are seeing, experiencing.

If you have not experienced this kind of transformation, then I ask you to step out of your fears just for a moment; let go and step away. Your Father is waiting to catch you. He is fully committed to you. He already paid for it. He already said, I will take your burden so you can walk freely with Me. Step. Let go. It's okay.

CHAPTER 19

No Performance Necessary

For God so loved the world that he gave his one and only Son, that whoever believes in him shall not perish but have eternal life.

John 3:16 NIV

When I held my baby girl in my arms for the first time, tears rolled down my cheeks. She was tiny. She was flawless, and I was her mom. Me. Messy, self-centered, me. Yet I was becoming a more mature, softer, and attentive version of me. I wasn't perfect, but does any mom step into motherhood with wholeness? I was being transformed. God was in the midst of writing my redemption story. All those little rays of God's Sonshine, all those *"Aha!"* moments I had experienced over the years were about to become bright. Illumination was coming.

Giving birth is filled with intense pain and crazy discomfort. However, in that moment when I held my baby, the memory of all the pain and discomfort I had just endured faded behind the beauty of what I was holding.

I believe this is the same for God. When we fully come to Him. When we trust Him. He holds us close. A tear rolls down His cheek, and all that pain from the cross vanishes. All that pain and discomfort Jesus endured was worth it to have you, to hold you.

> *He himself bore our sins in his body on the tree, that we might die to sin and live to righteousness. By his wounds you have been healed.*
>
> *1 Peter 2:24 ESV*

Our children are not precious to us because of something they did. As mothers, we don't hold our baby and think you are good because you just did a terrific job of slipping out of the womb. No, when our baby is placed in our arms for the first time and in the days that follow, we look at that tiny creature, and all that pain becomes worth it. The fact that you cannot sit or bend over is nothing compared to having that little life in your arms and bringing her home.

Likewise, God loves His children. They don't need to perform some task flawlessly to gain His love. He loves. He sees value and worth not because of anything His children have done or ever will do. It is the price He paid. It is a fading of all pain in the moment when He can hold you and call you His. The pain He endured was worth it. His tremendous agony brought you home with Him.

God Often Uses the Messed Up

So Jesus said to the Jews who had believed him, "If you abide in my word, you are truly my disciples, and you will know the truth, and the truth will set you free."

John 8:32 ESV

As I continued my journey, my husband was moved by God to create a Bible reading plan. I was a little taken aback and ashamed at first as I had never read through the entire Bible myself.

I had grown up in church, yet I never remembered being encouraged to read through the Bible. I felt like I wasn't smart enough to read all of the Bible. There were many books I didn't understand: Leviticus, Revelation, parts of Daniel, Isaiah, Song of Solomon, Romans and many others. What is God even trying to communicate to us now in the 21st century? Reading those books was confusing and discouraging. I had basically decided reading the full Bible was for theologians or people like my husband who spent hours studying the Scriptures.

So here I was, living with a man who had a vision to create a Bible reading plan for people just like me: the discouraged and tuned out. My husband's vision was to create a plan that caused less burn out and discouragement by making it less intimidating and get people reading through the Bible together. This wasn't intended to be a solo journey but a journey of life and encouragement, and one that would nourish an environment of accountability and growth.

Over the course of many months, a plan was formed that was Old Testament chronological with the New Testament interwoven. A two-year plan with only ten minutes of reading per day. When it was completed, I was relieved. All right, great, I thought I can now have my husband back in the evenings. Well, not quite. My dear husband had more ideas. He wanted us to read through the plan together and create questions for each day's reading as we went along. So much for me flying under the radar. The next two years we faithfully read, discussed, and created questions every night amidst a busy life that included my husband's full work schedule, raising a toddler, being pregnant with baby number two, an intense surgery for my husband, and having a challenging tongue-tied baby. Together, and only by the grace and strength of God, we came up with nearly 3000 questions.

Despite all the stress of that season, I was completely changed by reading through the Bible. Things I hadn't understood became clear. The heart and character of God was fully displayed throughout the entire Bible. I felt like I knew God in a whole new way. He became more real and more alive to me than ever before.

When I finished the reading plan, I was not served a diploma. I was not any smarter. However, I gained confidence in my Christian walk. Sure, there are absolutely still things I do not understand in the Bible. What I did gain, what I do understand is God's great, unfailing love for all people, God's unchanging character, and God's ability to use a lot of flawed and messy people. The Sonshine opened my eyes to the truth that God is not seeking out the perfected. God is not looking for the cream of the crop to accomplish His will. He is using the outcasts, the hot-tempered, the lonely, the oppressed, and even the proud. He can use me, and He can use you. You don't need to be a neat package. You don't need to be cleaned up for God. All you need to be is willing. Willing to go where He leads. Willing to listen and obey.

Your word is a lamp to my feet and a light to my path.

Psalm 119:105 NKJV

If you haven't, I encourage you to read through the Bible. Be changed by the love and character of God. You can see our Bible-reading plan and all the questions we made by going to https://BibleStudyTogether.com.

CHAPTER 21

Letting Go
of the Facade

Praise the Lord, my soul, and forget not all his benefits—who forgives all your sins and heals all your diseases, who redeems your life from the pit and crowns you with love and compassion, who satisfies your desires with good things so that your youth is renewed like the eagle's.

Psalm 103:2-5 NIV

Parenting is a continual reflection of God's love. From birth through the many seasons of childhood, there are things that as parents we are continually learning and discovering. Because of these tiny creatures, I began taking better care of my body, and therefore, the temple of the living God. For the first time, I was nourishing body and soul. The regular thoughts of purging and not eating were gone. Those defeated struggles disappeared by the grace of God after the experience of life growing inside me and the birth of a new God-formed creation.

I can't say it all just vanished; however, the daily fight did. Yes, from time to time I still struggle with body image. Yet, I walk in victory because that is not who I am or who I am becoming.

Having four pregnancies in six years takes a toll on the body. It is no wonder I am self-conscious at times. I can't control the stretch marks, loose tummy, or spider veins left after four babies, but I can control my reaction. I choose to praise God for these little lives instead of hating my body. I choose to see the work God is doing in my heart and my family's hearts instead of the scars and pain. I choose to acknowledge the beauty instead of calling it ugly as our society does. I choose to embrace my role as a mother rather than fight and resist the time, energy, and sacrifices parenting requires.

Parenting is rigorous, and therefore it has been the number one tool God is using to sculpt this heart since our first baby girl was born. I experienced some dark days after my first, but I realized the darkness was different this time. The dark is still dark, yet I had hope. Hope that this was temporary and there would be better days. Hope because I was not alone. I now had a personal, trusting relationship with my God, my Father. I had full confidence He was going to help me, grow me, and mature me. The past experiences had built my faith enough to allow my heart to stay open to Him.

The first five months with my firstborn baby girl were trying. She cried a lot for seemingly no reason. Night and day I would hold her as she cried, and I cried too.

The first year of a baby's life is often painted as glamorous and wonderful, however, that has not been my experience. It was difficult between the changing hormones, the excessive milk production, the healing from a massive tear, the crying, the lack of sleep, the dreams of them sleeping soundly next to you crushed, the screaming in the car seat, and so on. Everything about having a baby turns any bit of a self-centered world upside down.

The heart of man plans his way, but the Lord establishes his steps.

Proverbs 16:9 ESV

Having and raising a child brings any thorn to the surface of a mother's heart. I do believe this is God's way of maturing us, perfecting us. Hidden sin and motherhood just cannot exist if we are truly honest with ourselves.

As a first-time mom I wanted my little girl to be happy and thriving. I wanted her to have all she needed. With each crying session, I broke inside because I could not seem to help her. I was her mother, and no matter what I tried, she often kept on crying. I was confused as to why I could not fix it all.

I soon began to realize I will never be able to fix every pain and bad situation she must face in life. That is not what I am here for. I am her mother, yes, but I am not her Creator or Savior. I am her mother: one to help lead her, equip her, and teach her. I will never be able to take away the pain. I can hold her hand and walk with her through it. I will never be able to fix her broken heart, but I can hold her, cry with her, let her talk, and lead her to the Savior who can heal. I am a mother. That is my role, my calling. A mother is important. A mother is valuable. However, a mother can never take the place of God. God is the Refuge, Healer, and Comforter we all need. I had to let go of any control I was trying to pretend I had. I had to choose to trust instead. Trust the Almighty God to comfort and heal.

Letting go
On my knees

My heart, soul, and mind
Humbly bow

King, Healer, Redeemer, Friend
What You are to me
All in all
Everything

Letting go
Freedom rings

The last weight
Off of me
Just me at Your feet

Lighter steps
Invade me

Letting go
A process
Day after day
Freedom seemed so far away

Then one day
The words a reality

Letting go
Just me and You
Freedom
Released

The weight
The chains
The darkness in me
At Your feet

Heart, mind, soul
Free of black dark
Full Sonlight

Letting go
The me of old passed away
Empty vessel at Your feet

Now filled up
With all of You
My King, Healer, Redeemer, Friend

The letting go of me
The freedom You give invades all of me
Released from dark grips
New life of Light within me

Light and Release

In him was life, and that life was the light of all mankind. The light shines in the darkness, and the darkness has not overcome it.

John 1:4-5 NIV

This climb out of the dark pit was never about holding on tight. It was about letting go and allowing Jesus to lift me up. I finally see it. I finally see the Light. An illumination that accumulated from all those little rays of Sonshine. All His candles came together, and I see. I can finally let go of it all, every past pain from childhood, every false identity, every confusing spiritual lie, every facade of control over my body. I can let go and watch it all fall into the darkness while I am completely illuminated, free, and at the top in the Light. I am released! Released from every pain and burden I carry.

Release does not mean life is easy. Release does not mean I never make mistakes. Release means freedom. Freedom to love and be loved. Freedom to admit failures and try again. Freedom to trust my God and Savior with everything from money to children to a home and relationships. I am released. I am free in the love of Christ. I am no longer in or controlled by the darkness. It has no power over me and cannot blind me as I remain in the Light. I am released from its grips because of the blood poured out on the cross. Because of the victory of His resurrection. Because of the persistent love of my Father who pursued me and reached out at every call from the dark pit.

God desires release and freedom for all. There is light. There is hope for you or your loved one in the dark pit even if it is only one light flicker or one small candle at a time. Acknowledge the light you have right now in this moment, and little by little, you will come into full Light, illumination. I have been given a testimony. A testimony of release: from dark pit to life with abundant hope. A journey that brought illumination one small ray of Sonshine at a time.

When Jesus spoke again to the people, he said, "I am the light of the world. Whoever follows me will never walk in darkness, but will have the light of life."

John 8:12 NIV

You can have it too. Continue to call out of the darkness in the sweet and powerful name of Jesus. He is listening. He is working. The victory is there: paid in full. God wants to bring you into the Light, the life with abundant hope.

My past does not define me
My past does not create me
My past is not all I am
A part of me
A piece of history
My past, just one piece
Not the whole puzzle
That is me
My past I will not deny
My past I will not hide
For it's a piece of me
And not all of me
My past is part of the mold
My past gives me shape
For it I shall not be ashamed

God gave me the past
And there it shall stay
For today is a new day
Of grace, of love
My past I shall remember
My past I shall keep there
For today is a new day
Of hope, of peace
To serve God in the present
And thank Him for the past
Whatever it was
It's a piece of me
That brought me where I am today

A PRAYER AS YOU CLOSE THIS BOOK:

Heavenly Father,

As this beloved one closes the pages of this book and walks into the reality of their life, I pray for Your guiding light upon them. May they see and know You are with them. Awaken their eyes to Your light shining even in their darkest and most painful circumstances.

Father, You have called us and are beckoning us to walk in the Light. Bring Your beloved into Your light. Press deeply the truth into their heart. Let any lies that suffocate and blind them fall away in the powerful name of Jesus. May full release illuminate this life.

You, oh Father, are the giver of life with abundant hope. May our hearts be receptive to Your gift. Open our eyes where they need opening. Give us the strength to let go and allow love and light in.

Father, I lift up Your beloved ones to You now that You may shine on them and light their path. Bring release from every chain. Bring redemption through Your name. Give the gift only You can give: life with abundant hope.

In the sweet and precious name of Jesus, Amen.

"The Lord bless you and keep you; the Lord make his face shine on you and be gracious to you; the Lord turn his face toward you and give you peace."

Numbers 6:24-26 NIV

GET HELP

If you or someone you know is struggling with depression or suicidal thoughts, reach out today. Contact a professional and start receiving the help and healing needed. It's okay to ask for help.

And I will lead the blind in a way that they do not know, in paths that they have not known I will guide them. I will turn the darkness before them into light, the rough places into level ground. These are the things I do, and I do not forsake them.

Isaiah 42:16 ESV

Need help connecting with God?

We will guide you how to daily read the Bible.

Bible Study
TOGETHER

650+ Maps   Mobile App   Study Journals

Daily Questions - Videos - Booklets - Much More

Prayer Manager   Private Groups

BIBLESTUDYTOGETHER.COM

Check it out today!

Made in the USA
Las Vegas, NV
14 July 2021